Knowledge *Blaster!* Guide to

Art History

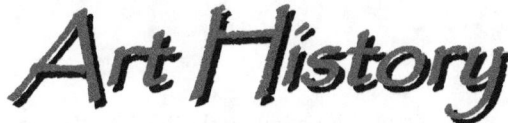

Yucca Road Productions

YRP

Dear Reader,

The *Knowledge BLASTER!* Series consists of books of general and academic interest, written with the specific intention of compressing a great mountain of available information into an easily digestible morsel. Every attempt has been made to simplify unwieldy material.

Where feasible, the books are patterned in an efficient question-and-answer mode in which answers become meaningful extensions of helpful, information-packed questions.

We hope you use this reference work as a launch pad to propel yourself into more in-depth studies. However, if you find this little book provides all the information you need, then consider your knowledge...
Blasted!

Knowledge BLASTER! Series
American History
Art History
Food and Drink
Geography and Travel
Literature
Movies
Music
Mythology
Sports
Weight Training and Total Fitness
World History

Yucca Road Productions

Contents

Art in the Old Stone Age

Around 15,000 BC, bison, deer, horses, and cattle were painted across the walls of a cave near Lascaux, France. In the same period, a more impressive painting of a wounded bison, with controlled shading and a more true-to-life, empathic feel of the animal's plight, was drawn in a cave near Altimira, in *this* country.
— Spain.

The Salisbury Plain in England is home to a circular grouping of large carved stone, over thirteen feet tall, that was assembled in the time span of 1800 to 1900 BC. The purpose of the megalithic ("large stone") monument was probably religious, with some orientation toward identifying specific days of the year. What is this early bit of architecture known as?
— Stonehenge

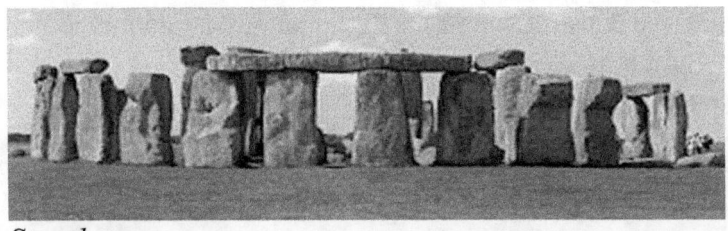

Stonehenge

What term is used to describe the art of the peoples of tropical Africa, the Americas, and the South Pacific, who use their art to trap powerful spirits, much as people of the Stone Age did?
— "Primitive."

As civilization began, some 6,000 years ago, along the Nile in Egypt and the Tigris and Euphrates Rivers of Mesopotamia, the object of man's art turned from the natural and spiritual toward that which more and more came to occupy his thoughts.
— Man himself.

Most of the creations that survive from early Egypt are depictions of, or monuments to, the royalty. These privileged few shared the concept of an afterlife that required complex burial chambers linked by shafts to square mounds faced with brick or stone. What are these forerunners of the pyramids called?
— Mestabas,

The age of pyramids climaxed around the Fourth Dynasty with the construction of the three famous, smooth-sided pyramids at...?
— Giza.

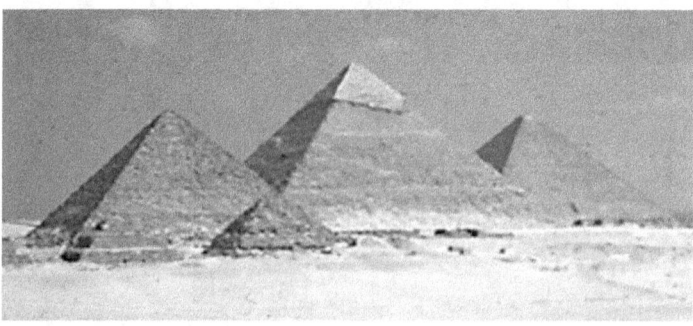

Egyptian pyramids

Much of what we know of ancient Egyptian art comes to us from the pyramids.

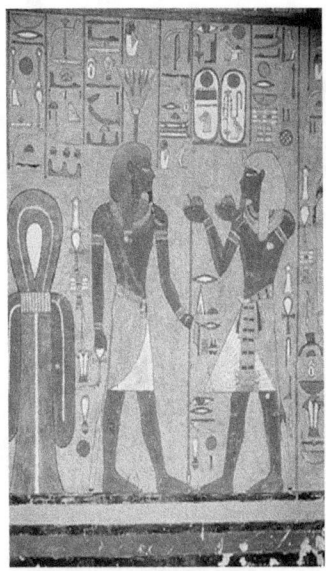

Egyptian wall art

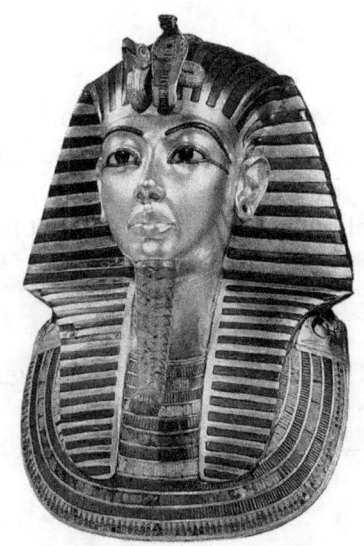

Mask of King Tut

Near the Giza pyramids stands a 65-foot tall statue of a lion with a pharaoh's head, called...?
— The Great Sphinx.

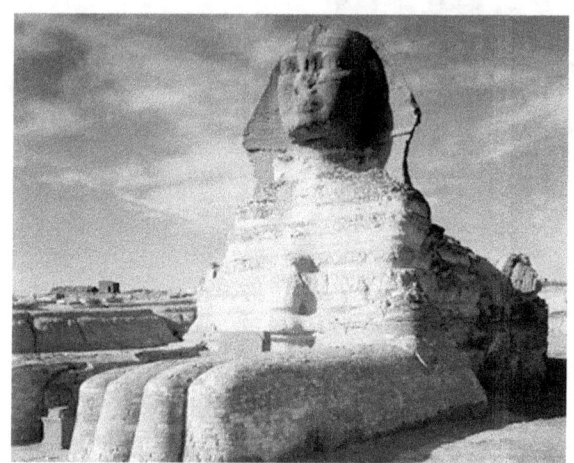

The Great Sphinx.

In Mesopotamia, the Sumerians laid out cities that stressed the dominant role of the temple to physical as well as spiritual existence. Some of these temples were built on platforms that grew to great heights. What are these monuments called?
— Ziggurats.

This most famous of the ziggurats, mentioned in the Bible, has been destroyed.
— The Tower of Babel, built by Nebuchadnezzar.

The Greeks

With the formation of Greek civilization (1100 to 700 BC) small sculptures and painted pottery saw full development of this style, based on triangles, checkers, and concentric circles.
— The Geometric.

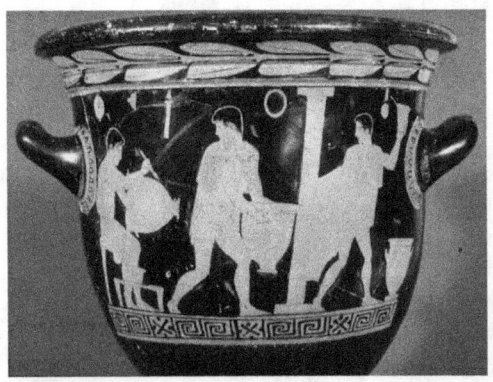

Greek pot

Greek "Archaic"style emerged from contact with Egypt and the Near East as trade ties grew. In the sixth century BC, vase painters began signing their works. Black- figure scenes incorporated human and animal forms in a narrative style. Toward 500 BC, the black figures were replaced by figures of this color.
— Red.

Around 480 BC, Greek artists began to fill a white background with sketched forms that began to take on three dimensions, with depth implied by foreshortening. This period saw the subjects changed from scenes of myth and legend, such as Hercules Strangling the Nemean Lion, to scenes that actually occurred, such as the defeat of King Darius of Persia by Alexander the Great. This time is known as...?

— The Classical Period, which lasted roughly from the age of Pericles to that of Alexander the Great.

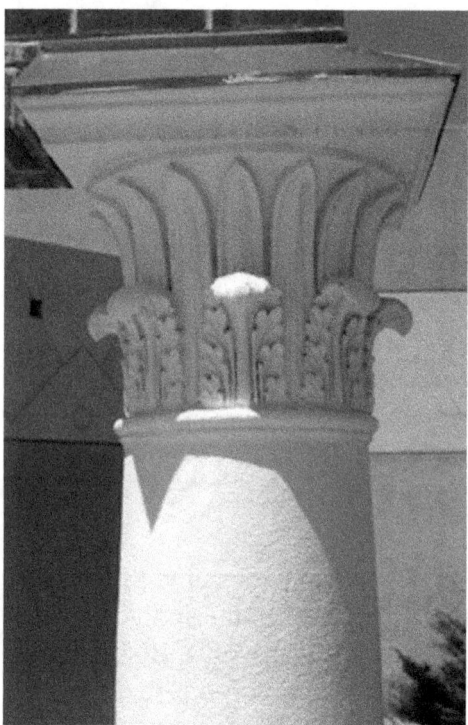

Greek column top

Most notable of the Greek artistic achievements were the temples, identified by "architectural order" as either Doric, Ionic, or...?
— Corinthian.

From ground up, Doric temples consist basically of the stepped platform, the columns, and this, which includes everything above the columns.
— The entablature.

Columns are made up of drum sections with vertical grooves (flukes) topped by this somewhat horizontal cap upon which rests the entablature.
— The capital.

The highly-sought piece of the entablature which exhibits the artistry of period sculptors, often done by the most highly skilled artisans as a showcase for their talents, is called a...?
— Frieze.

What single feature of the Ionic order of architecture is lacking in the earlier Doric order?
— Ionic columns were set upon a distinct base. Corinthian columns also have a base, and are distinguished by ornate capitals with stylized acanthus leaves.

This temple, in Athens, is usually considered the apex of Greek Classical architecture, with refinements of proportion and line that give it an aesthetically pleasing grace and ease. Its grand scale is belied by tricks of illusion, such as steps that curve slightly upward toward the middle, and corner columns that are a bit closer to their neighbors than the others. The temple, built on a hill called the Acropolis, is titled...?
— The Parthenon.

Athenian architects, who developed the Ionic order about 450 BC, constructed the smaller temple of Athena Nike with more slender columns resting on...?
— Bases (unlike Doric columns).

In the history of sculpture, the Greeks were the first to completely free figures from the surrounding stone— the

characters stood by themselves! A late seventh-century BC statue, free-standing, of a Greek youth is called a...?
— Kouros.

In Classical Greek sculpture, figures in action seemed firmly grounded, and figures in repose maintained a supposition of possible movement. This style, however, was an Athenian trait, and when the Peloponnesian War brought the polis of Sparta to power, crippling Athenian might, the Classical style lingered in various forms of degeneration for three centuries. Artistic styles of the Mediterranean world regressed in this post-Classical style, known as...?
— Hellenistic.

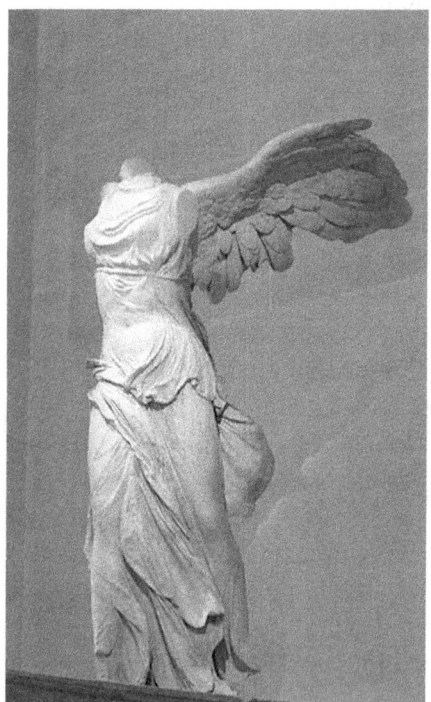

Perhaps the greatest work of Hellenistic sculpture is this winged goddess of victory, straining into the wind, found headless in the coastal waters.
— The Nike of Samothrace.

Nike (or Winged Victory) of Samothrace

The Romans

Just as the Romans were great admirers and imitators of Greek art, so too were they indebted to this earlier culture for their architectural prowess.
— The Etruscans.

As Roman power spread around the shores of the Mediterranean, new cities were built to house the colonial governments. Etruscan influence is shown by extensive use of this feature, an overhead curve made of wedge-shaped blocks that hold each other in place.
— The true arch.

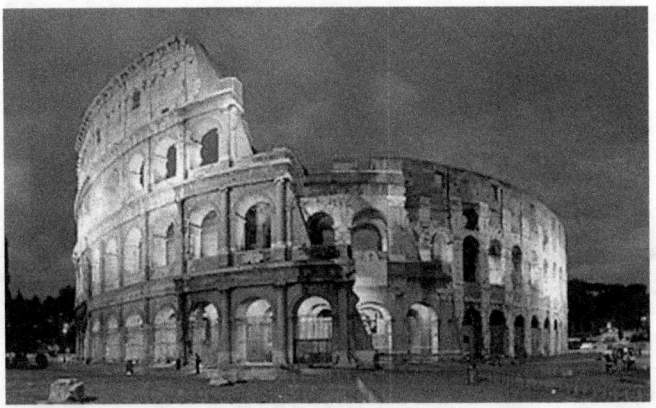

The Colosseum in Rome

This enormous circular structure in Rome, originally known as the Flavian Amphitheater, is a prime example of

the Roman arch and the vaulting systems derived from it. Fifty thousand spectators could view the arena from its seats.
— The Colosseum, built around 80 AD.

This huge round Roman temple, topped by an enormous dome, was dedicated to all the gods.
— The Pantheon.

The 79 AD eruption of Mount Vesuvius destroyed the life of this city, but left for posterity much evidence of Roman art.
— Pompeii.

Many interiors of Pompeii, such as the Ixion Room from the House of Vettii, were decorated in the technique of painting on fresh plaster, known as...?
— Fresco.

Middle Ages

Artistic emphasis shifted once again, in the Middle Ages, in order to express that which occupied man's mind. In Rome, Christianity was legalized in 313 AD by the Edict of Milan and was the state religion by 395. Intricate wall mosaics using tesserae of glass depicted Biblical scenes on the walls of Christian churches. Illustrated Bibles were made possible by the development of parchment paper and this thin, bleached animal hide.
— Vellum.

The new writing materials allowed for development of the type of book we still use today, known technically as a...?
— Codex.

Important churches built in the reign of Roman Emperor Justinian include San Vitale in Ravenna, Italy, and this famous one in Constantinople, the Church of the Holy Wisdom, or...?
— Hagia Sophia.

Basic parts of the church, or basilica, were standardized by a council at Charlemagne's capital of Aachen, 816-817 AD. In part, these consisted of a central nave (the main body, between the side aisles) and the transept, which projected from the main body at right angles on either side to form a...?
— Cross.

This recess, usually semicircular with a half dome, formed the eastern or altar end of a church.
— The apse.

From the thirteenth to the fifteenth century, medieval art of the Goths, or barbarians, rose in prominence. Gothic buildings were soaring structures with pointed arches. All that was not Gothic reflected the Roman style of round-arched, solid, heavy architecture and was called...?
— Romanesque. (Until around 1200).

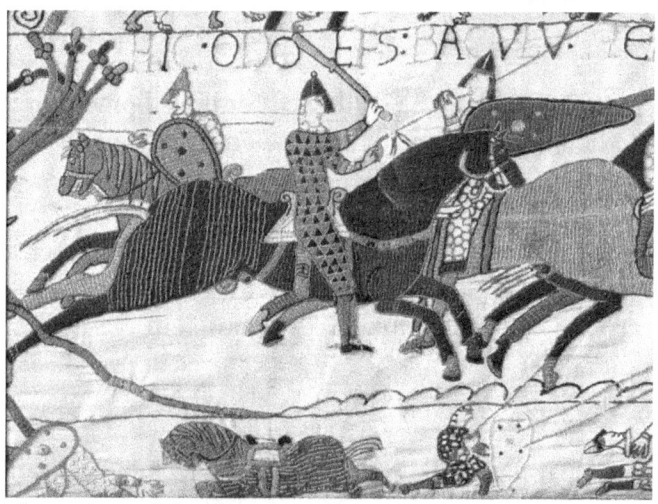

A portion of the Bayeaux Tapestry

Romanesque painting and other art was lacking in subtleties of perspective and shading, but nonetheless conveyed scenes that were readily understandable. This 230-feet strip of cloth is embroidered with details of

William the Conqueror's invasion of England, including
the fateful Battle of Hastings.
— The Bayeaux Tapestry.

What name is commonly given to the bell tower of the
Cathedral complex of Pisa, Italy, constructed 1053 to
1272, whose weak foundation caused it to tilt after
construction?
— The Leaning Tower of Pisa.

This cathedral (whose name means "Our Lady") was
begun in 1163, in Paris. It added the use of flying
buttresses to the Gothic style.
— Notre Dame.

The town hall of Florence, Italy, although Gothic, is a
grim, fortress-like building known as...?
— The Palazzo Vecchio.

The Renaissance

In the 1330s the Italian poet Petrarch, himself an embodiment of humanism and individualism, set a pattern for the development of a new direction in thinking, and thus in art, that carried mankind out of the Middle Ages. Acknowledging the death of the Greco-Roman world, the humanists studied history, languages, philosophy, and literature outside the religious framework of the past, and put aside conventions in an attempt to surpass them. This "rebirth" of the intellect is known by the French term...?
— "Renaissance."

The Renaissance of painting and sculpture is thought to have begun in this Italian city in the early 1400s.
— Florence.

Perhaps the greatest sculptor of the fifteenth century, this Florentine revived the Classical counterpoise that gave his subjects a dynamic realism. His works include *St. George*,

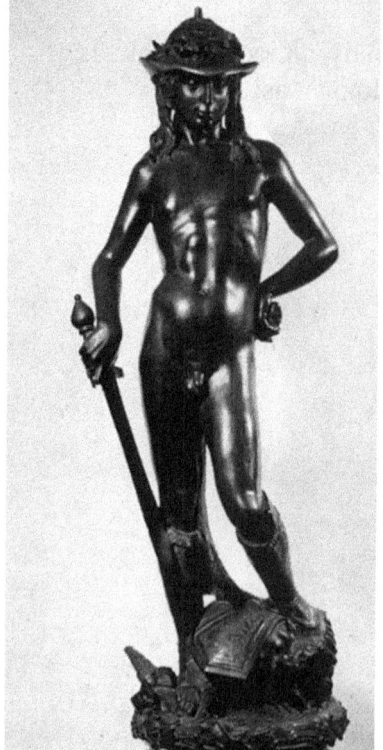

Donatello's David

Zuccone, and a bronze *David*— the first full-sized, free-standing nude figure since before the Middle Ages. His bronze *Equestrian Monument of Gattamelata* still stands in Padua.
— Donatello

After Donatello left Florence, Lorenzo Ghiberti sculpted Baptistery doors which demonstrates mastery of this principle that systematically diminishes the size of figures in relation to their distance from the viewer.
— Scientific perspective.

Sandro Botticelli was the last of the great Early Renaissance painters of Florence. His *The Birth of Venus* was done for an associate of Lorenzo the Magnificent, who was an avid patron of the arts and head of this powerful family.
— The Medici.

The artistic leap in this Northern country is regarded by some as a Renaissance streak of new realism and by others as "late Gothic."
— The Netherlands (especially Flanders).

In Flanders, the Master of Flémalle was among the first to abandon tempera (in which the pigments were mixed with egg yolk) in favor of slow-drying and blendable oils. Oils could yield a wide range of effects, from thin glazes to thick, heavy-bodied creams called...?
— Impasto.

The Master of Flémalle (probably Robert Campin) showed an emerging mastery of perspective that had eluded earlier artists. Jan van Eyck used a lessening of

contrast along with a subtle emergence of light blue-gray to denote distance from the viewer, so that far mountains merged with the sky. This optical illusion is known as...?
— "Atmospheric perspective."

This Dutch artist conveyed weird, irrational images, some of which remain inexplicable. Perhaps best known is his triptych (on three panels) *The Garden of Delights*.
— Hieronymous Bosch.

The fifteenth century saw the development of printing, allowing mass production and distribution of images for the first time, in this country.
— Germany.

Leonardo, Michelangelo, Raphael, Titian, and Bramante produced the key works of *this* period between 1495 and 1520.
— The High Renaissance.

At this point in history, humanist emphasis on the importance of the individual brought forth the notion of

daVinci's Mona Lisa del Gioconda

the ideal person, the universal genius who could accomplish any feat by application of knowledge and talent. This was the "Renaissance man," perhaps best exemplified by this Italian artist and inventor.
— Leonardo da Vinci.

da Vinci's great unfinished *Adoration of the Magi*, in Florence, implied three-dimensional bodies with this method, whose name means "light and dark."
— Chiaroscuro.

Leonardo's *The Last Supper* was painted in this city.
— Milan.

Returning to Florence after the Medici had been dispelled, Leonardo produced his most famous portrait, of... *someone* (whose true identity is still a matter of dispute.)
— *The Mona Lisa.*

Michelangelo's statue of David, commissioned in 1501, adorned the entrance to Florence's Palazzo Vecchio. Called to Rome by Pope Julius II to build an enormous tomb, he grudgingly accepted Julius' commission to paint the ceiling of this chapel, since he considered painting a lesser art. He worked on the job for four years, finishing in 1512.
— The Sistine Chapel. (*The Creation of Adam*, where God's outstretched hand touches that of his Creation, is the most famous scene depicted there in fresco).

More than twenty years later, Michelangelo was called back to the Sistine Chapel, to paint an end wall, and produced this grim masterpiece.
— *The Last Judgement.*

Julius II wanted a church in Rome that would overshadow any other. Donato Bramante drew up the original design in 1506, and, after Bramante's death, Raphael and Michelangelo modified the original to create what we know as...?
— St. Peter's.

After the deaths of the Bellinis, with whom he had studied, this man was considered the finest painter in Venice. In 1518 he completed the famous altarpiece of the *Assumption of the Virgin*. For the rest of his career he was sought after by the rulers of Europe. His works include *Rape of Europa, Sacred and Profane Love*, and *Christ Crowned With Thorns* (1542).
— Titian.

Following the High Renaissance, for 75 years the style known as _____ dominated, exemplified by Tintoretto and El Greco. Figures became contorted, scale and spatial relationships confused.
— Mannerism.

In sculpture, the era of mannerism was reflected by Cellini and by this creator of *The Rape of the Sabine Women*.
— Giovanni Bologna.

In Germany, early sixteenth century art was dominated by Matthias Grunewald's paintings and the woodcuts and engravings of this famous printmaker.
— Albrecht Dürer

The Netherlands produced Northern Europe's major painters of the Late Renaissance. This master explored

moral choices with his *Land of Cockayne*, depicting men who have become slaves to their appetites. In 1565, he showed man's relations to the seasons in his *The Return of the Hunters*.
—Peter Bruegel the Elder.

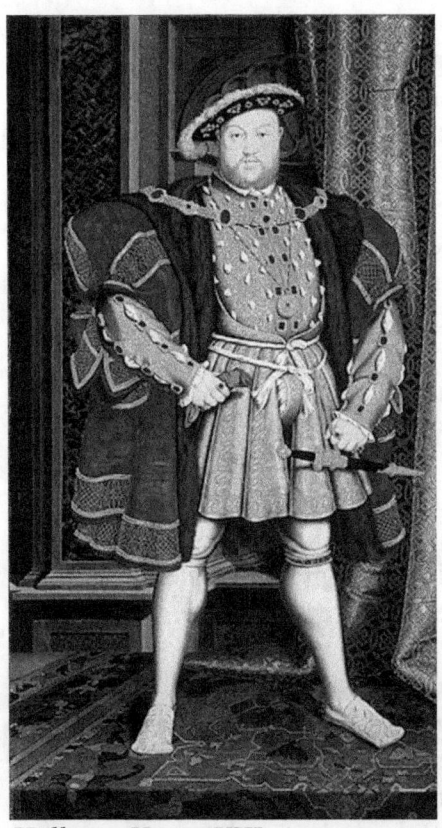

He illustrated Erasmus' In Praise of Folly, in Switzerland, before doing a portrait of England's Sir Thomas More. Court painter of Henry VIII, he painted many portraits of the king and his wives.
— Hans Holbein the Younger.

Holbein: Henry VIII

The Baroque

Out of the Renaissance came a sophisticated style that marked the period from 1600 to 1750. Called the Baroque style, it resulted from the widespread familiarity with linear and atmospheric perspective, chiaroscuro, anatomy, new materials, and architectural principles that Renaissance artists pioneered.

Rome was its birthplace (and Caravaggio its prime exponent), but the Baroque spread quickly. Flemish painter Peter Paul Rubens (*Peasant Dance*) studied in Italy for eight years, and then settled in Antwerp as court painter for the Spanish regent. Rubens' chief assistant gained fame as a portraitist and became court painter in England, 1632-41. He was...?
— Anthony van Dyck.

Rubens helped to advance the technique of this Spanish court painter as well, allowing him to produce such masterful group portraits as *The Maids of Honor.*
— Diego Velasquez.

France, under the guidance of Louis XIV, had replaced Rome as the center of art by the late seventeenth century. Nicholas Poussin, the greatest French painter of the era, took this subject which Bologna had sculpted and gave to it breath and drama.
— *The Rape of the Sabine Women.*

Louis XIV's first great architectural project was the completion of the Louvre, a palace begun more than a century earlier. His greatest enterprise was this vast and ornate palace, just outside Paris.
— The Palace of Versailles.

The Dutch masters were products of the Baroque as well. Franz Hals, with his robust *The Jolly Toper*, and this greatest genius of the region, typified the style.
— Rembrandt. His *Self-Portrait*, *The Polish Rider*, and *The Night Watch* are the most famous.

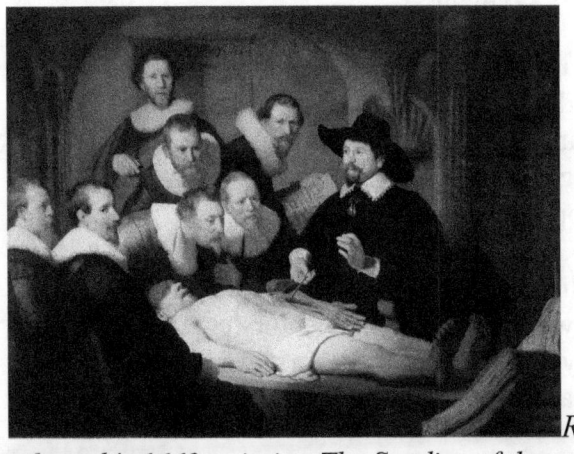Re

mbrandt's 1662 painting The Syndics of the Drapers' Guild

Rococo

Invented in France around 1700, the Rococo style is denoted by fanciful, lacy motifs and delicately executed ornamentation.

Antoine Watteau included figures of Classical mythology in his depictions of everyday characters, as in *A Pilgrimage to Cythera*. Perhaps the best painter of the Rococo style, this artist's figures are typified in *Bathers*.
— Jean Honoré Fragonard.

After the Great Fire destroyed much of London in 1666, this architect designed more than fifty of the churches that were rebuilt, including the monumental St. Paul's, of the Church of England.
— Sir Christopher Wren.

The first English painter of great importance since the Middle Ages was this eighteenth century creator of "morality plays" on canvas, social criticisms that delight the eye, such as *The Harlot's Progress* and *The Rake's Progress*.
— William Hogarth.

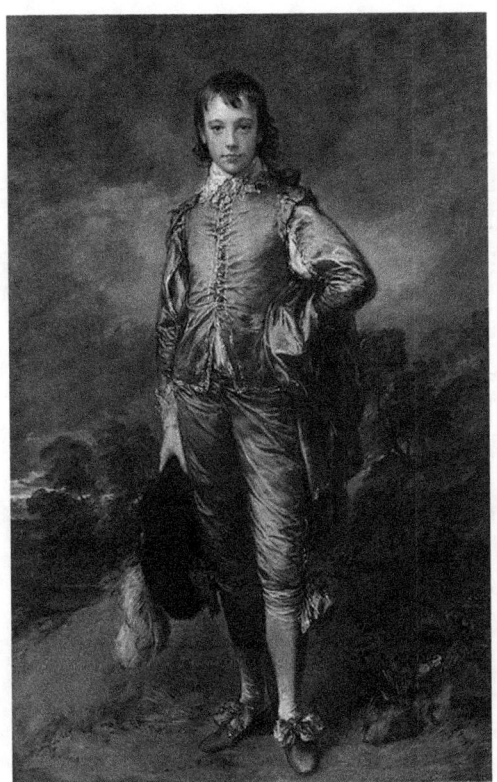

Thomas Gainesborough's Blue Boy

In this same period, Thomas Gainesborough painted *Mrs. Siddons* and *Blue Boy*, and this creator of *Mrs. Siddons as the Tragic Muse* formulated rules of painting in his *Discourses*.
— Sir Joshua Reynolds.

Art in the Modern World

Neoclassicism of the late eighteenth century was a revival of Greek style. The Doric columns of this imposing gate in Berlin were designed by Karl Langhans.
— The Brandenburg Gate.

This French artist painted *The Death of Socrates* in 1787 and *The Death of Marat* (a political leader of the French Revolution) six years later.
— Jacques Louis David.

This Pennsylvanian caused a sensation in 1760 as the first American artist to visit Rome. His frontier pride showed in his work, even after he settled in London, as can be seen in *The Death of General Wolfe*.
— Benjamin West.

An echo of the Enlightenment, this art style of the mid-eighteenth to mid-nineteenth centuries showed a trend toward emotional expression that gave the movement its name.
— Romanticism.

Art and architecture in the Romantic period borrowed much from past movements. Renaissance styles were revived in the early nineteenth century, and then this last phase, which lingered past 1900, appeared.
— Neo-Baroque, such as the design of the Paris Opera.

This Spanish artist documented the execution of a group
of Madrid citizens by the occupying French troops of
Napoleon in his *The Third of May, 1808.*
— Francisco Goya.

This Frenchman's rendering of *The Third-Class Carriage*,
showing people grouped closely but each alone in their
thoughts, belies his earlier career as a cartoonist.
— Honoré Daumier.

Francois Millet painted French landscapes and scenes of
rural life, such as *The Sower.* He was one of a handful of
artists who had settled in the village near Paris that gave
this group its name.
— The Barbizon School.

This English Romantic painter concentrated on developing
a broad, free technique to show the sweeping forces of
nature in his many landscapes.
— John Constable.

France produced one great landscapist in the Romantic
period, who traveled the Italian countryside for his subject
matter.
— Camille Corot.

Realism and Impressionism

In a denouncement of Romanticism, Gustave Courbet condemned the use of subjects drawn from history, mythology, and religion, saying, "I cannot paint an angel because I have never seen one." In 1849, he put his feelings to canvas with *The Stone Breakers*, showing two men working on a road. The style was called...?
— Realism.

Edouard Manet's _____ __ ___ _____ portrays two gentlemen, fully clothed, picnicking with a woman who is nude for no apparent reason. Manet had chosen to combine elements that were aesthetically pleasing, despite their lack of plausibility as an actual event. His works had a profound impact on Impressionists.
— *Luncheon on the Grass*.

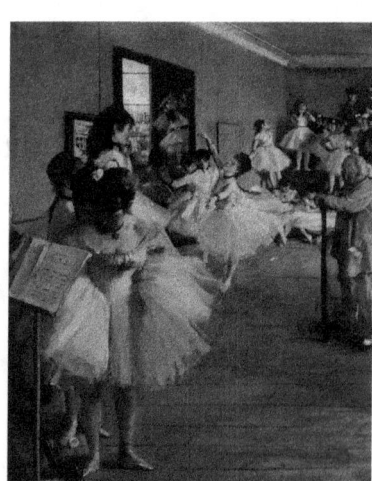

Degas painted many scenes of dancers

This realist is best known for his transcriptions of ballet dancers, on stage, at rehearsal, and in the dressing room. With his contemporaries of the 1850s and '60s, he pushed for purer color, using a method of placing patches of color side by side instead of blending them (a concept

called "the revolution of the color patch," attributed
primarily to Manet.)
— Edgar Degas.

Among the last of the Realists, this artist's use of color
patches brought a liveliness to his group of flirting couples
in *Le Moulin de la Galette*, his *Boatmen's Lunch*, and his
Three Bathers with a Crab.
— Auguste Renoir.

In 1850s London the "Pre-Raphaelite Brotherhood"
declared that they would paint pictures of substance,
observing nature, ignoring conventions and taking
inspiration from the "primitive" masters of the fifteenth
century. On the whole, they produced no great works, but
their words reflect the desire of many artists of the time to
split with tradition.

The Impressionists followed the lead of the Realists in
portraying subjects drawn from real life, but in searching
for more scientific or immediate ways of conveying their
truths, the art became misty and vague.

Claude Monet and Camille Pissarro dissolved solid
objects in favor of showing the play of light upon them.
The Impressionists no longer mixed colors exactly on the
palette, but juxtaposed pigments on the canvas so that the
viewer's eye was allowed to do the mixing, as in
pointillism, divisionism, and broken color.

Painting members of her own family, <u>she</u> revealed subtle
clues of alienation among them. Manet may have actually
helped her rework some of her art; she married his brother.
— Berthe Morisot.

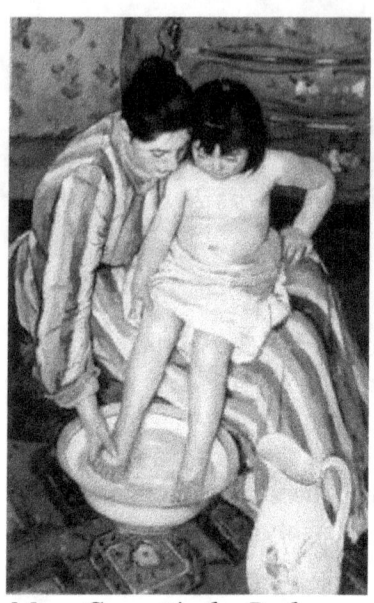

Mary Cassatt's the Bath 1891

Besides Morisot, this American (who spent most of her life in France) was the only woman to gain fame as a master of the new coloring. As in *The Bath*, most of her paintings are inspired by maternal instincts.
— Mary Cassatt.

Winslow Homer and Thomas Eakins were outstanding among American Impressionists. This Paris- trained American painted "decorative" pictures, and was accused by British critic John Ruskin of "flinging a pot of paint in the public's face."
— James Abbott McNeill Whistler.

The creased surfaces of this sculptor's works of bronze produce ever-changing plays of light. His *The Thinker*, finished in 1889, is his most recognized work.
— Auguste Rodin.

In America, this group of Realists, led by Robert Henri, came to notice in 1908.
— The Ash-Can School. Most notable of "The Eight" ashcanners was John Sloan.

The Revolt Against Realism— Post-Impressionism and The Fauves

Along with the rise of Sigmund Freud's psychoanalysis at the turn of the century, art began to focus inward on the human character. Artists began to distort their portrayals of realistic objects in an attempt to convey their own inner vision. This was called...?
— Expressionism.

Bringing together nature and abstraction, this French painter became a world leader whose work, after his 1906 death, turned the waters back on the Impressionists and provided a platform on which later cubists, abstractionists and Fauves might stand. He thought that all natural forms could be based on the cone, the sphere, and the cylinder.
— Paul Cézanne.

With Cézanne and Van Gogh, this was one of the three original Post-Impressionist masters. In 1883, he abandoned his stock-brokerage, his family, and security to take up painting. He took his decorative method to Tahiti after the bills piled up (and a rumored murder attempt by Van Gogh.)
— Paul Gauguin, who was known as a Symbolist.

This Frenchman (1844-1910) was hailed as foremost of the modern "primitives." As a customs inspector, he found time to paint only on Sundays. His decorative works reflect his lack of training but are fresh and imaginative, such as *Scene on the Seine*.
— Henri Rousseau.

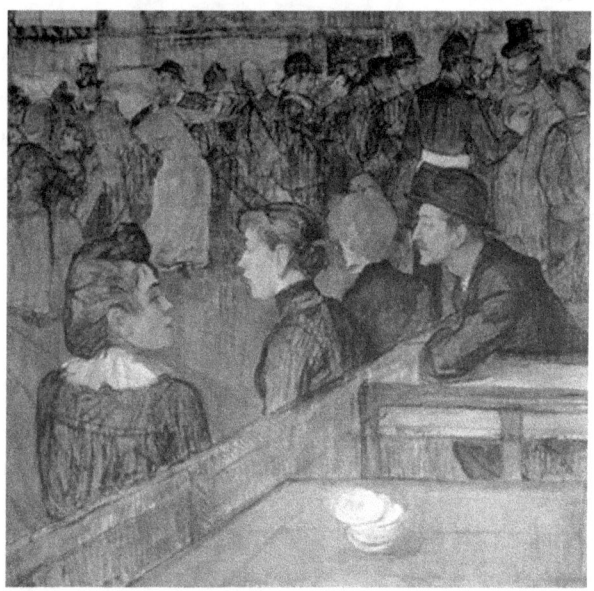

Henri de Toulouse-Lautrec

A dwarf, this French artist portrayed characters from his own life in the nightspots of Paris, giving the customers and performers a joyless and oppressive demeanor.
— Henri de Toulouse-Lautrec. He painted *At the Moulin Rouge* in 1892.

This Norwegian's stark style gave an image of nightmarish fear to his character in *The Scream*, 1893.
— Edvard Munch.

Important among Post-Impressionists were Aristide Maillol (*Seated Woman*, 1901), Wilhelm Lehmbruck (*Standing Youth*, 1913), and Ernest Barlach (*Man Drawing a Sword*, 1911).

Among American primitives, this sign-painting preacher is best known for his many versions of one subject, *The Peaceable Kingdom*.
— Edward Hicks.

Most popular among American primitives in the 1940s was Anna Mary Robertson Moses. After a life of hard farm labor, she took up painting in her seventies and became known as...?
— Grandma Moses.

Famous for his type of divisionist system, known as pointillism, he built up areas of color with dots of various pigments. But his arrangement of linear elements and recessive planes (as shown in *Sunday on Grande Jatte Island*) may be the true mark of his genius.
— Georges Seurat.

In 1905, a room was assigned at a Paris gallery for the exhibition of a group of unknowns which included Henri Matisse, Georges Rouault, Georges Braque, and Raoul Dufy. Very shortly, the room became known as the "cage aux fauves"— the cage of the wild beasts. The Fauves became international leaders of the art scene and continued as such well into the 1940s.

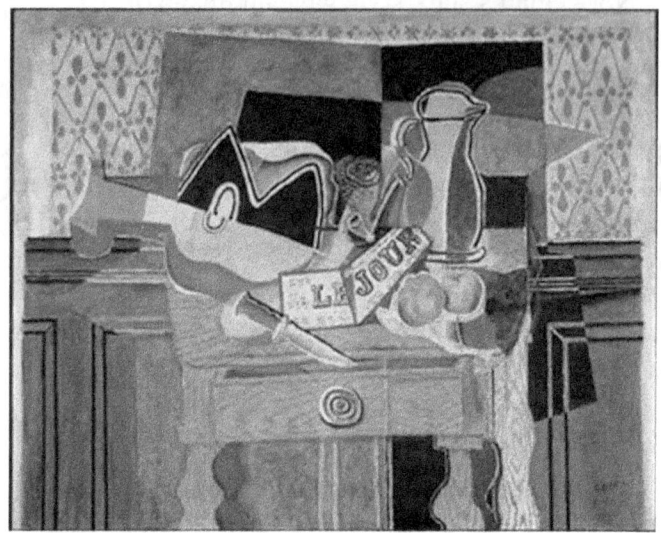

Georges Braque's Still Life Le Jour, 1929

Of the Fauves, Braque is credited with beginning the cubist use of planes and volumes to demonstrate perspective, a technique used by this man in his *The Demoiselles of Avignon (1907)*.
— Pablo Picasso.

Among the Fauves (also known as the School of Paris), this innovator's abstract personal style used machine parts (bolts, cylinders, rods, etc.) to portray his visions.
— Fernand Léger, who painted *The City* in 1919.

With Matisse and Picasso, this artist was among the "Big Three" of the Fauves, but he soon went his own way, applying heavy outlines, dark backgrounds, and color like that of stained-glass windows to his message- bearing themes. He gave his characters emotion, as in *The Old Clown*, a merry-maker whose age has left him serious and morose.

— Georges Rouault.

Other Schools and Styles

A group of painters in Dresden, Germany, formed in 1905 a Fauve-like society known as...?
— The Bridge.

Although not a member of the Bridge, this Austrian echoed their ideals, rejecting the refinements of the Romanticists in paintings such as his *Self-Portrait* of 1913.
— Oskar Kokoschka.

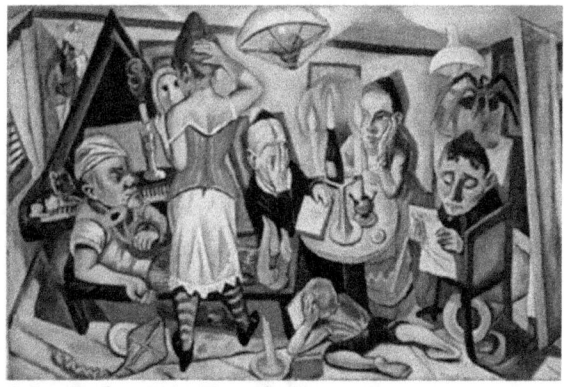

Max Bekman's Family Picture

This Bridge descendant, painter of the disquieting triptych *Departure*, completed the painting on leaving Germany under Nazi pressure in 1933.
— Max Beckmann.

Arriving in Paris in 1910, this Russian Jew began painting memories of his childhood. A forerunner of surrealism, he portrayed subject matter from Jewish life and folklore in a manner suggestive of fairy tales. In 1945, he designed costumes for Stravinsky's ballet, *The Firebird*.
— Marc Chagall.

This Russian, a leader of the Munich group called the Blue Horseman, abandoned representation altogether after 1910. His nonobjective abstractions were titled with terms borrowed from the music world (as were Whistler's).
— Wassily Kandinsky.

Piet Mondrian, a Hollander, with Theo van Doesburg, founded the _____ group at Leiden in 1917, painting in in complete non-objectivism
— De Stijl.

During World War I, this German-Swiss painter devised a pictorial method of his own to condense complex ideas about civilization. In *Twittering Machine* and *Park near Lucerne* the viewer sums up the simple lines and shapes, possibly, only after reading the intriguing title.
— Paul Klee.

This Frenchman, along with Max Ernst, launched a movement called Dadaism during World War I, preaching non-sense and displaying ready-made objects such as bottle racks and snow shovels. The name "dada," French for "hobby horse," was supposedly picked at random from a dictionary. He was...?
— Marcel Duchamp.

This successor to Dadaism was founded in 1924 by poet André Breton. Distorting time and space in a dream-like way, Salvador Dali, Max Ernst, and Joan Miró (Dog Barking at the Moon, 1926) produced its most striking examples.
— Surrealism.

In America, this photographer was the driving force behind the modernist movement. Among the most original of his group was painter Georgia O'Keefe, whom he married in 1924.
— Alfred Stieglitz.

By the 1920s, the Expressionist movement in the New World was centered in Mexico. After the fall of the dictator Porfirio Dias in the Mexican Revolution of 1911, a group of young painters expressed the spirit of the Revolution in vast public murals incorporating the heritage of pre-Columbian art.

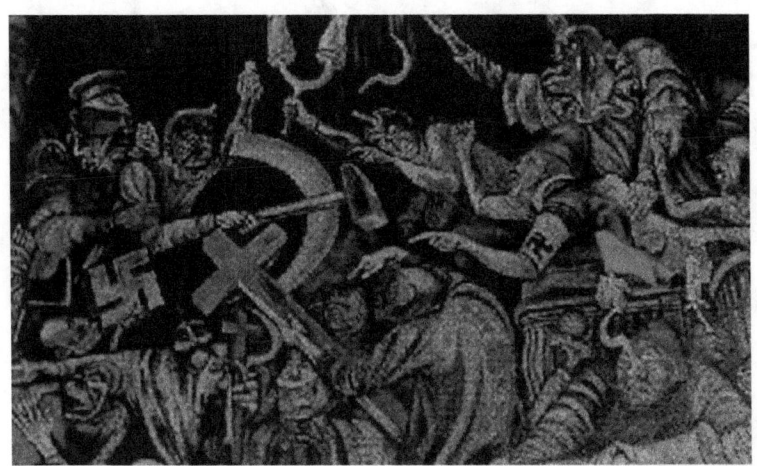

Orozco's The Clowns

This muralist painted *Victims* as part of a mural cycle at the University of Guadalajara, in 1936.
— José Clemente Orozco.

In the years following World War II, Abstract Expressionism, or Action Painting, arose from Surrealism, pioneered by this Armenian immigrant to America. His *The Liver is the Cock's Comb* shows a host of objects, each apparently in the process of turning into something else.
— Arshile Gorky.

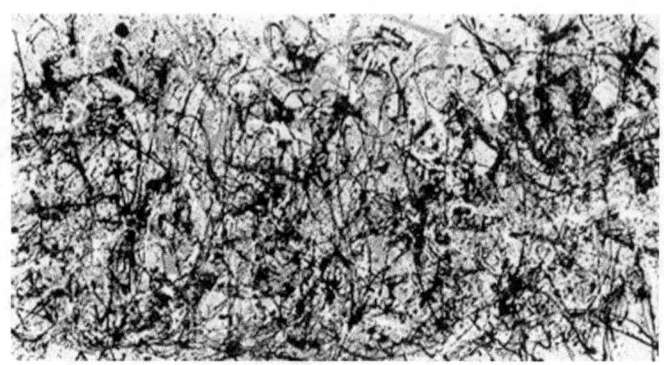

Pollock's Autumn Rhythm

In 1950, this Action Painter's huge picture, *One*, created a stir. Its colors were dripped or flung onto the canvas instead of applied by brush.
— Jackson Pollock (dubbed "Jack the Dripper.")

Pollock's wife succeeded in reintroducing the figure into Abstract Expressionism. She had never given up the brush as a tool, and in her Celebration the tangled, energetic lines hint at actual body shapes.
— Lee Krasner.

Victor Vasarely, Josef Albers, and Richard Anuszkiewicz contributed greatly to this trend of painting images designed to trick our vision with optical illusions, (such as Vasarely's *Vega*, an alternately bulging and shrinking checkerboard.)
— Op Art.

A spin-off of Pop Art is Photo Realism, in which objects are drawn to photographic perfection, although grouped or transposed in such a manner as to baffle the eye.

Examples are *Queen* by Audrey Flack and *New Shoes for H* by...?
— Don Eddy, 1973.

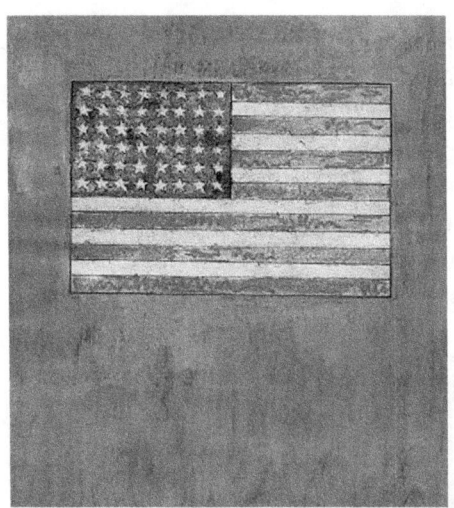

Jasper Johns' Flag on Orange Field, 1957

Among pioneers of Pop Art are American Jasper Johns (*Three Flags*, 1958) and this artist, whose canvases resemble huge comic strips.
— Roy Lichtenstein.

William de Kooning and Jean Dubuffet were among the Action Painters as well, and this artist helped transform the movement into a style called Color-Field Painting. His *Earth and Green* consists of two rectangles, red over green, outlined in purple.
— Mark Rothko.

Mark Rothko, Untitled 1951

Modern Architecture

Chicago's Louis Sullivan, the first great modern architect of the 1900s, originated the dictum, "form follows function." His outstanding disciple designed suburban dwellings called "Prairie Houses" that blended with the flat landscape around them. His "Falling Waters" house in Pennsylvania, built on a cantilever over a stream, was a ground-breaking triumph.
— Frank Lloyd Wright.

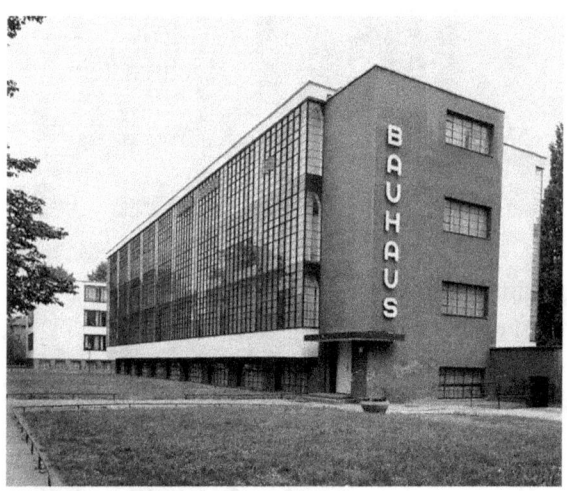

Walter Gropius' Bauhaus

What German architect illustrated the "International Style of the 1920s" with a group of buildings constructed for the

Bauhaus school of art and architecture at Dessau?
— Walter Gropius.

This French architect called his houses "machines to be lived in," such as the famous Savoye House. On a more ambitious scale, he designed the main buildings for the capital of the Punjab, Chandigarh, and the Visual Arts Center at Harvard (1961-62)
— Charles Édouard Le Corbusier.

Who designed the Seagram Building in New York, 1958?
— Ludwig Mies van der Rohe.

Whose school of architecture has campuses in Arizona and Wisconsin?
— Frank Lloyd Wright.

From 1619 to 1642, this man was the architect to England's James I and Charles I.
— Enigo Jones.

This co-designer of Central Park planned Stanford University's Palo Alto campus.
— Frederick Law

This Finnish-American innovator designed the circular chapel and concrete dome of the chapel of Massachusetts Institute of Technology. He also did the Trans World Airlines Terminal in New York, the General Motors Technical Center in Warren, Michigan, and the Dulles International Airport in Chantilly, Virginia.
— Eero Saarinen.

A wedge-shaped "keystone" is inserted last in an...?
— Arch.

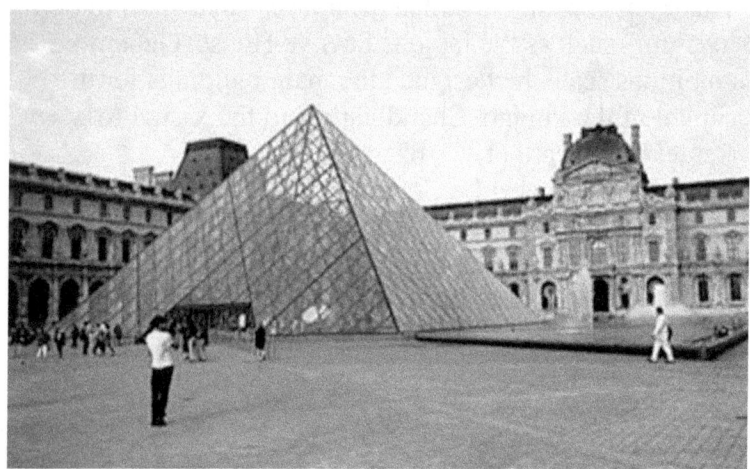

I.M. Pei: entrance to the Louvre, in Paris

A Chinese-American architect, his works include the East
Wing of the National Gallery of Art in Washington, D.C.,
the West Wing of the Museum of Fine Arts in Boston, and
a subterranean entrance complex for the Louvre in Paris
that is topped with a glass pyramid.
— I. M. Pei.

These water spouts at the tops of buildings are carved in
shapes of grotesque beasts.
— Gargoyles.

This structure usually tops a rotunda.
— A dome.

What is the slim tower on a mosque called?
— A minaret.

The Gothic style of architecture, which followed the
_____, featured ribbed vaults and flying buttresses.
— Romanesque.

All classical orders of columns except the Greek _____
have a base.
— Doric.

This beautiful building in Agra, India, is the tomb for
Mogul emperor Shah Jahan.
— The Taj Mahal.

What building contains the Freedom Statue?
— The US Capitol.

Photography: Art through Technology

Joseph Niepce is the French inventor usually cited as the creator of the first photograph, in 1822. He joined forces with this man, who improved the camera and chemical processes.
— Louis Daguerre

In the 1830s, this Englishman invented a photographic process wherein positives could be made from a paper negative.
— William Henry Fox Talbot.

Many of France's leading citizens, including Sarah Bernhardt, posed for this photographer in the 1850s.
— Nadar (real name Gaspard Tournachon.)

The American Civil War was the subject of this man's team of photographers, which included Alexander Gardner.
— Matthew Brady. (Gardner became an outstanding photographer in his own right.)

In *The Two Paths of Life*, this photographer posed actors to portray a young man's choosing between virtue and vice. The photo told a story, while at the same time providing an artistic scene in a Romantic vein, proving that the camera could be an artistic tool.
— Oscar Rejlander.

The Secessionist movement of the 1890s sought to prove that photography was art, experimenting with the development process to produce aesthetic works. This man, a supporter of modern art in America, opened the Photo-secession gallery, in New York in 1902.
— Alfred Stieglitz.

This young man, backed by Stieglitz, exhibited his photo of the sculptor Rodin contemplating *The Thinker* (with his sculpture of Victor Hugo looking on) in 1902.
— Edward Steichen.

Eadweard Muybridge studied animal locomotion, making a set of photos of a trotting horse, in 1877, pioneering the field of...?
— Motion photography.

In 1907, this Frenchman introduced color photography.
— Louis Lumiére

Soon after taking up photography, in 1932, this former cubist painter became the most significant photojournalist of his time, although his Surrealist techniques distinguish him as an artist.
— Henri Cartier-Bresson.

Showing mundane objects, such as his *Pepper*, 1930, in tight close-up with great detail, this photographer fused realism and abstraction.
— Edward Weston.

The first staff photographer of Fortune and later working for Life magazine, this woman had a keen eye for composition, turning architectural shots into art in the '30s

and '40s. Her photos of poor Americans in the South and elsewhere are still studied by photographers today.
— Margaret Bourke-White.

He made "Rayographs" by placing objects directly on photographic paper before exposure.
— Man Ray.

This English painter has been making exemplary photographic collages since 1982.
— David Hockney.

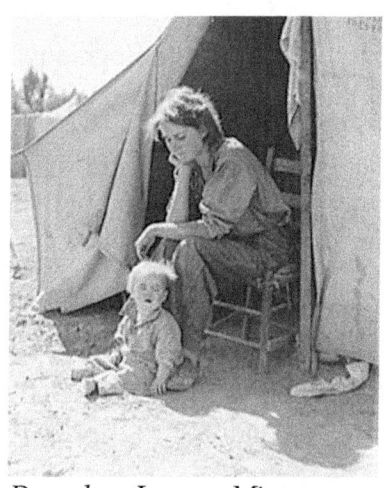

Dorothea Lange: Migrant Mother, California, 1936

As a documentary photographer during the Depression, this lady used her camera to convey the poverty and grief of the time. Her *Migrant Mother,* California, 1936, caused the government to rush food to starving migrant workers.
— Dorothea Lange

Artists in Books and Movies

Andy Warhol called his biography...?
— *Famous for 15 Minutes*.

What artist was portrayed in the book and film, *Lust for Life*?
— Vincent Van Gogh.

Who was portrayed by Charlton Heston in *The Agony and the Ecstasy*?
— Michelangelo.

Somerset Maugham's book, *The Moon and Sixpence*, told of this artist's pilgrimage to Tahiti.
— Paul Gauguin.

This group of heroic crime-fighters chose their names in honor of four of the greatest artists of all time.
— Teenage Mutant Ninja Turtles.

The Chelsea Girls (1966) is one of this artist's quirky films.
— Andy Warhol.

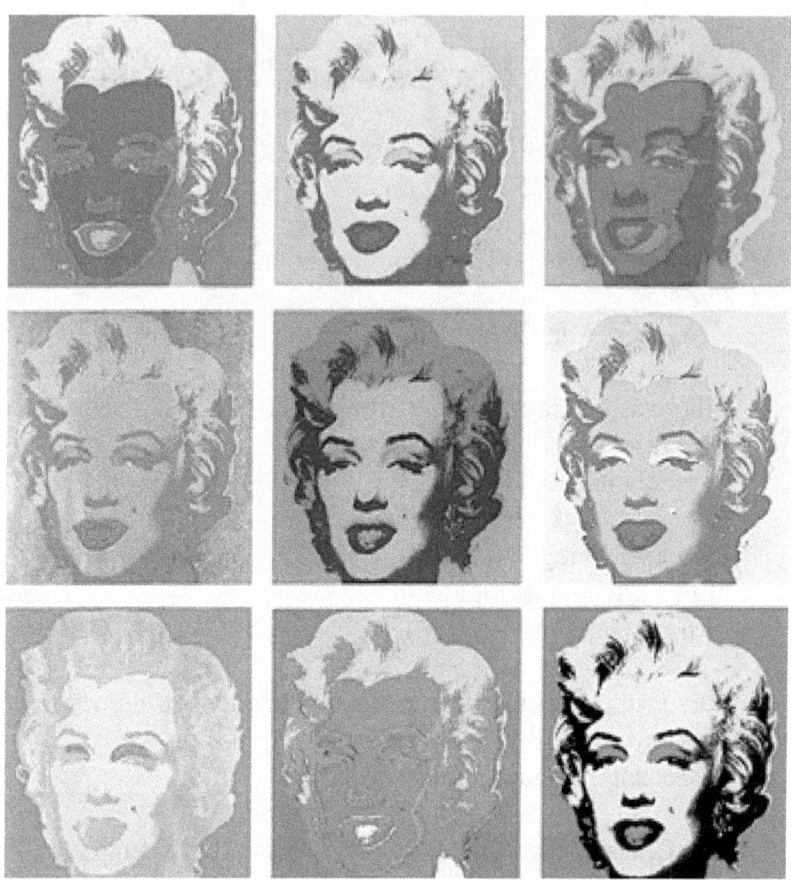

Andy Warhol's treatment of Marilyn Monroe

A Question of Technique

What are the primary colors of pigmentation?
— Red, yellow, and blue. (In the study of light, red, green, and blue are considered primary.)

Aquarelle is another name for...?
— Watercolor.

These colored chalklike sticks are most often associated with soft hues, but can be quite brilliant colors.
— Pastels.

What name is given to the bits of colored glass or marble that are used in mosaics?
— Tessarae.

What would you be admiring if you handled Worcester, Spode, or Wedgewood?
— Types of china.

This German city is renowned for its china.
— Dresden.

What European town lends its name to a type of pottery?
— Delft, the Netherlands. (Not all Delft is made there.)

Antique Majolica pottery is often this color.
— Cobalt blue.

Mother-of-pearl was often used to decorate this tough material of paper pulp, in Victorian times.
— Papier-mâché.

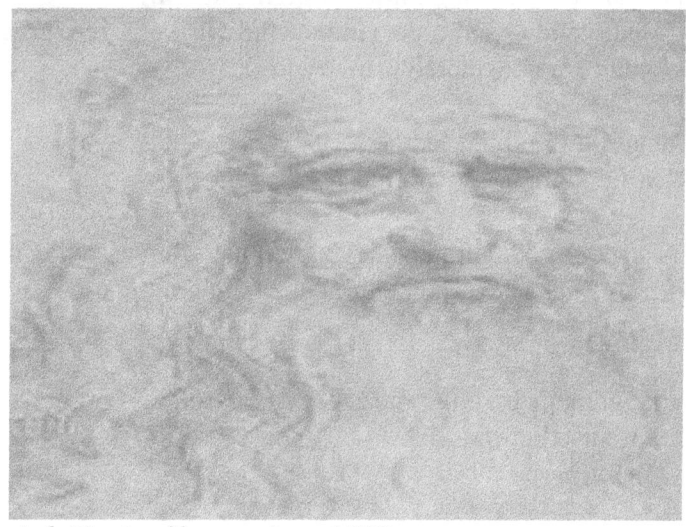

A daVinci self portrait, c. 1512

In painting, subtle, misty transitions in tone are referred to by this term. The technique, whose name means "Smoke-like," is usually attributed to da Vinci.
— Sfumato.

The use of light and shadow to dramatize elements of a painting is called...?
— Chiaroscuro.

What term generally refers to the art of the Olmec, Maya, and Aztec civilizations?
— Pre-Columbian.

What term is used to describe mobile and moving art?
— Kinetic art.

Artists and Their Works

Gilbert Stuart's most famous portrait subject was...?
— George Washington.

What western artist illustrated, in 1888, a series of magazine articles written by Theodore Roosevelt?
— Frederick Remington.

Which Wyeth followed N.C.and Andrew?
— Jamie, Andrew's son.

Which Wyeth is famous for the "Helga" paintings?
— Andrew, son of N. C. *Christina's World* is his best-known.

Whose dripping method is represented in *Number One, Lavender Mist* and *Autumn Rhythm* (1950)?
— Jackson Pollack's. (Time magazine called this abstract expressionist "Jack the Dripper.")

Famous for pictures of Coke bottles, Campbell's soup cans, and Marilyn Monroe, this pop artist received a degree in pictorial design from Carnegie Tech in Pittsburgh, in 1949.
— Andy Warhol.

Who painted *The Four Freedoms*?
— Norman Rockwell.

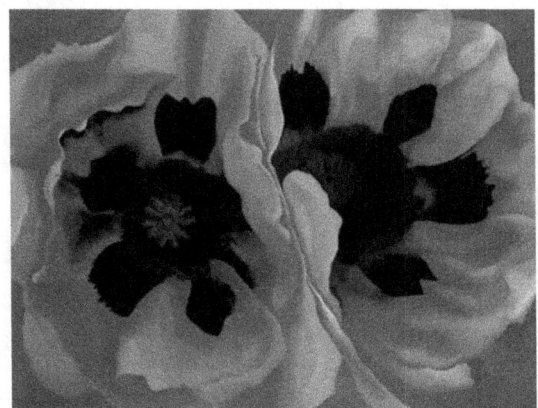

O'Keefe's Oriental Poppies

This artist was the wife of renowned photographer Alfred Stieglitz.
— Georgia O'Keefe. (His photo of her hands sold, in 1983, for $398,500.)

Rockwell Kent's bold black-and-white illustrations of the 1920s and '30s exemplified this art style.
— Art deco.

The sunny climate of Los Angeles, where he settled in the 1960s, has influenced the pop art and other contrivances of...?
— David Hockney.

This portraitist is supposed to have said, "Every time I paint a portrait, I lose a friend."
— John Singer Sargent.

John James Audubon, painter of *The Birds of America* in the 1830s, studied under...?
— Jacques-Louis David.

This painter of *American Gothic*, the often-parodied picture of an overly-serious farmer and spouse with pitchfork, taught fine arts at the University of Iowa in the 1930s.
— Grant Wood.

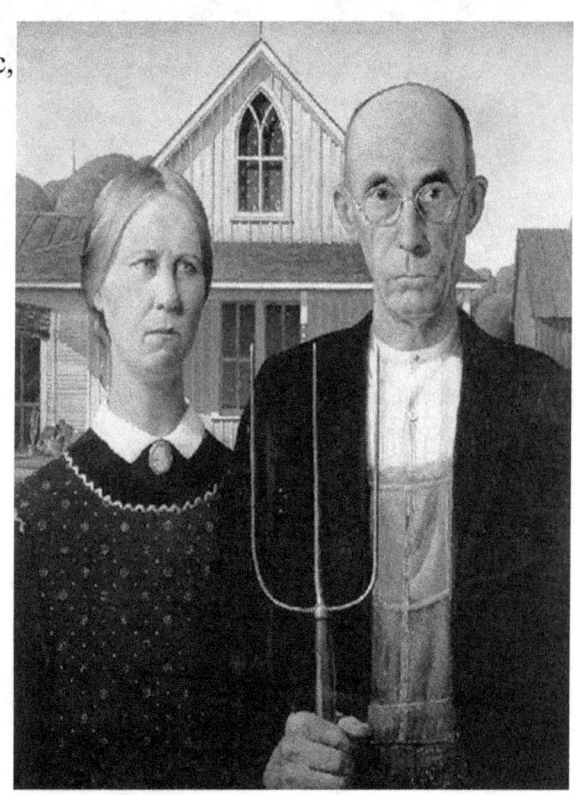

Grant Wood's American Gothic

At the age of 76, New York-born Anna Mary Robinson's arthritis interfered with her embroidering and so she took up painting. By what name is Ms. Robinson better known?
— Grandma Moses.

What musical instruments are featured in *Spirit of '76*?
— The fife and the drum.

In reference to this American impressionist, Degas said, "I will not admit that a woman can draw so well."
— Mary Cassatt.

Famous for his depictions of ocean-related subjects, this New Englander painted *Incoming Tide, Scarboro, Maine*, in 1883.
— Winslow Homer.

As Homer is famous for seascapes and Sargent is famous for portraits, John Constable is known for...?
— Landscapes.

Arrangement in Gray and Black was painted by... ?
— James Whistler. (The painting is better known as "Whistler's Mother.")

This Italian is noted for his portraits of long-necked women.
— Amedeo Modigliani.

How many characters appear in Leonardo da Vinci's *Last Supper*, painted on a Milan wall?
— Thirteen. (Leonardo's *Adoration of the Magi* altarpiece was painted in Florence, but never completed.)

Though he considered himself a sculptor, he was commissioned by Pope Julius II to paint the Sistine Chapel ceiling. The resulting paintings, including the *Creation of Adam*, are considered among the world's best.

Many years later, he was called upon by Pope Paul III to paint *The Last Judgement* on the end wall of the Chapel.
— Michelangelo, (whose last name was Buonarotti. His father, Lodovico Buonarotti, was mayor of the village of Caprese, where he was born in 1475.)

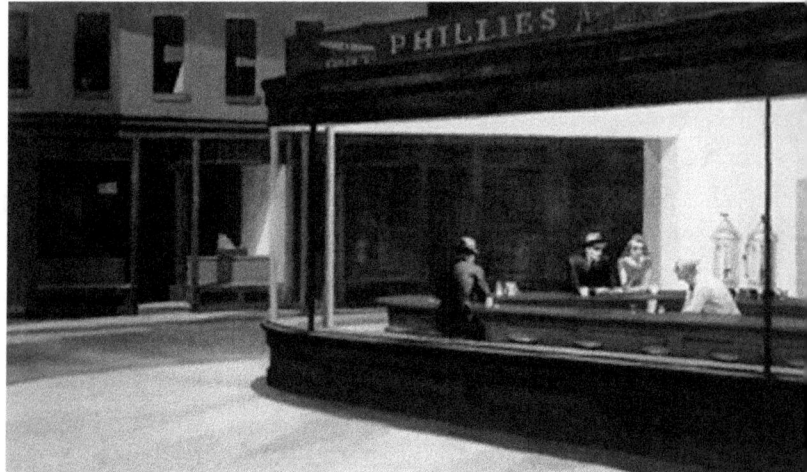

Night Hawks by Edward Hopper

Nighthawks was this American's stark painting of a diner, inspired by a Greenwich Avenue restaurant.
— Edward Hopper.

Famous for his drooping watches, this Spanish Surrealist painted *An Andalusian Dog* and *The Golden Age*. With Luis Bunuel, he made two Surrealist films. His *Persistence of Memory* is better known as "Soft Watches."
— Salvador Dali. He is buried at his museum in Figueras, Spain.

This artist's *View of the Rialto* is filled with waterborne gondolas.
— Francesco Guardi.

Born in 1746, this Spaniard called his home, "The House of the Deaf Man." He painted the Dutchess of Alba and was called before the Spanish Inquisition because of his painting, *The Naked Maja*. In the 1780s, he painted the Marquesa de Pontejos in a Marie Antionette-like shepherdess costume.
— Goya.

Thomas Gainesborough's *Master Jonathan Buttall* is better known as...
— "The Blue Boy."

"Soft" sculpture was invented by Claes Oldenberg, a native of...?
— Switzerland.

Picasso's daughter was named for the dove he created for a 1949 Peace Conference. She has made a name for herself as a designer of fine jewelry.
— Paloma Picasso.

This French colleague of Picasso, one of the developers of Fauvism, made contributions to the development of Cubism.
— Georges Braque. (His friendship with Picasso ended with the advent of World War I.)

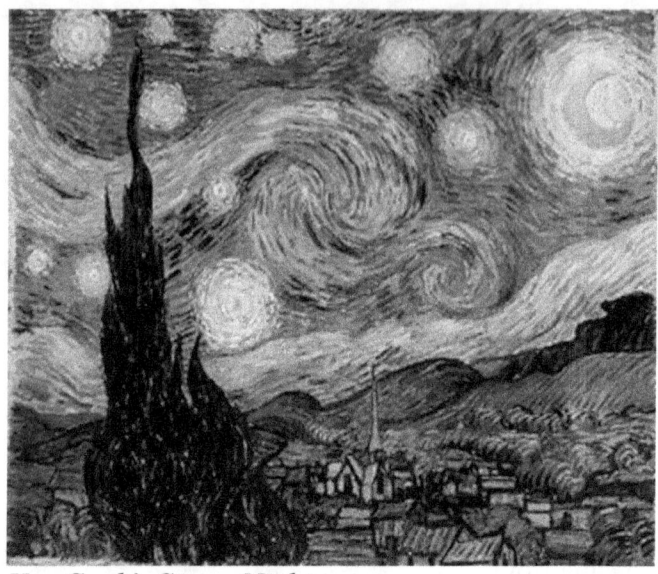

Van Gogh's Starry Night

Who painted *The Night Café*? (He painted *Starry Night* while in an asylum in France and is said to have sold only one picture, *The Potato Eaters*, in his lifetime.) — Vincent Van Gogh. Six months after his 1890 suicide, his devoted brother Theo, who often supported him, died.

Famous as a Cubist, this artist designed scenery and costumes for Cocteau and Massine's ballet, *Parade*. He painted harlequins and circus performers in his "rose period." His *Guernica* (an abstraction of the horrors of war) was completed in about a month, with the help of his mistress, Dora Maar. He unveiled his painting *Three Musicians* in 1921, and died in 1973 at the age of 91. — Pablo Picasso.

This muralist is from Mexico. His works deal with
Mexican life, history, and social problems. He was
married to noted artist Frida Kahlo.
— Diego Rivera.

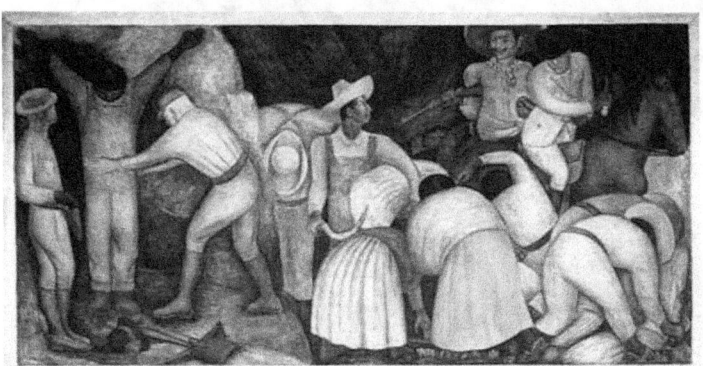

Rivera: The Exploiters, 1926

Edvard Munch (pronounced "moonk") was a modern
artist from_____. His emotionally charged works include
The Shriek (or *The Scream*), *Vampire*, and *The Kiss*, all
done in the 1890s.
— Norway.

What Swiss painter, who describes his work as "taking a
line for a walk," studied in Munich and toured Italy before
returning to his native land to make his etchings?
— Paul Klee.

Famed for his watercolor landscapes, Albert Namatjira
is...?
— An Australian aborigine.

Before his 1898 death, at age 26, this Englishman became famous for his black and white art Nouveau.
— Aubrey Beardsley.

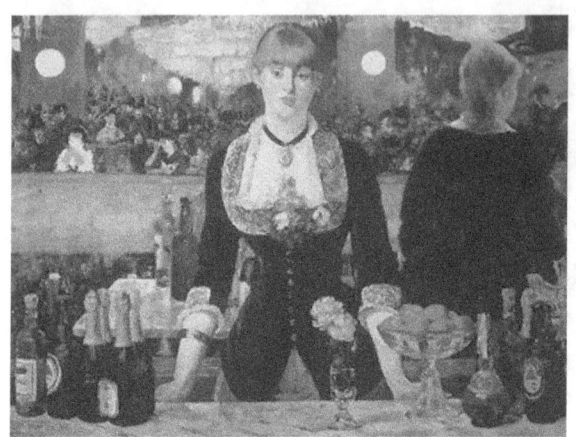

Manet's Le Bar aux Folies-Bergere, 1881

Who painted *Concert in Touilleries Garden*? (The 1867 execution of Emperor Maximillian of Mexico inspired one of his few historical paintings.)
— Manet.

Romain de Tirtoff was an art deco designer better known as...?
— Arty.

This artist's pointillist technique was as yet not perfected when he painted *A Bathing Place*, around 1884. The last impressionist exhibition featured his *Sunday Afternoon on the Island of Grande Jatte.*
— Seurat.

This Russian-French artist, who died in 1985, painted *The Rabbi of Vitebsk*. In 1967, he became the first living 20th Century artist to have an exhibit in the Louvre.
— Marc Chagall.

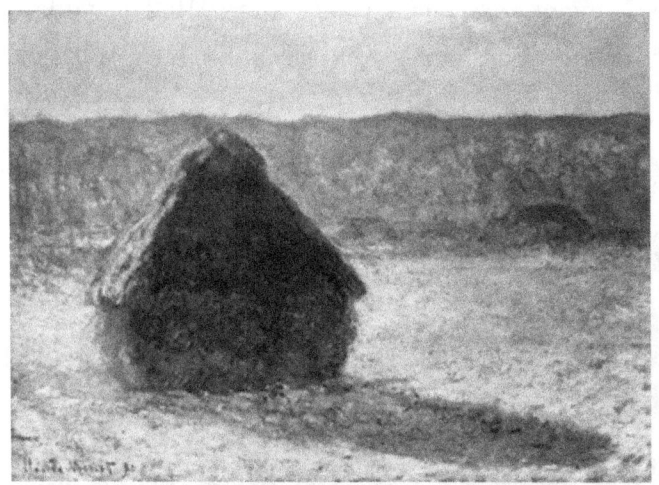

One of Monet's haystacks

His name is often confused with Manet. A founder of Impressionism, he is considered an outstanding figure in landscape painting. Though blind, he made renderings of water lillies, among other things.
— Claude Monet.

Before this French impressionist became known for his studies of ballerinas and racing scenes, he painted historical scenes.
— Degas.

Sculptor Raymond Duchamp-Villon was the older brother of this artist who gained fame in the Dada movement.
— Marcell Duchamp.

In his characteristic wild, primitive style, this Frenchman did his *Tropical Forest with Monkeys* in 1910. His works, such as *The Sleeping Gypsy*, influenced the Surrealists.
— Rousseau.

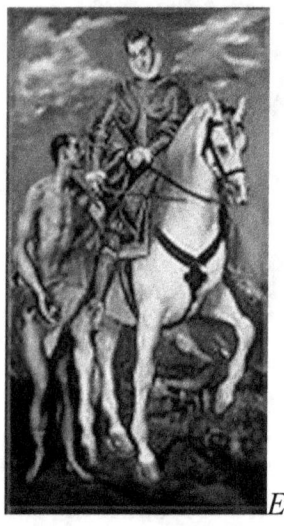

l Greco: Saint Martin and the Beggar

Domenico Theotokopoulos was born in Crete, studied in Titian's studio in Venice, and, after 1580, settled in Toledo in Spain. His *View of Toledo* is perhaps his most easily recognized work. In the *Laocoon*, the artist portrays a priest of Troy, who cautioned against accepting the Wooden Horse. By what name is Theotokopoulos better known?
— El Greco.

The Venitian artist Tintoretto depicted this patron saint of Venice.
— St. Mark.

Who designed macabre woodcuts known as *Dance of Death*?
— Hans Holbein the Younger. He became the court painter of English king Henry VIII.

Death and the Miser and *Garden of Earthly Delights* were two paintings with interesting names by this artist with an interesting name.
— Hieronymous Bosch.

In this artist's 1872 painting of Pont Neuf, Paris' oldest bridge, his brother Edmond is shown in two places.
— Renoir.

What nickname was given to the French Rococo painter, Fraginard?
— Frago.

This Dutchman's paintings on biblical themes include *The Descent from the Cross* and *The Blinding of Samson*. His *Joseph Accused by Potiphar's Wife* is based on Genesis.
— Rembrandt. Many of his portraits are of his wife, Saskia.

Museums and Galleries

In what country is the Prado?
— Spain.

Where is the Tate Gallery?
— England.

Michelangelo's 14' statue of David can be found in the Galleria dellàccademia of this Italian city, known as "The Cradle of the Renaissance."
— Florence.

This palace in Florence is home to the Silver Museum.
— Pitti Palace.

Where is the Doge's palace, wherein the frescoes of Gentile da Fabriano were completed by Pisanello?
— In Venice.

The Birth of Venus is in the Boticelli room of this Florentine palace.
— The Uffizi.

This former home to France's kings was converted to a museum in 1793, after the palace was moved to Versailles. Today its many famous art objects include *Venus de Milo*.
— The Louvre.

In 1993, a wing of the Louvre was dedicated to this historic Cardinal.
— Richelieu.

Many of the treasures of Pompeii are housed in this Italian city's Museo Archeologico Nazionale.
— Naples.

Where is the Butler Institute of American Art?
— Youngstown, Ohio.

This permanent art work in Texas features ten half-buried autos.
— The Cadillac Ranch.

This prominent oil man and philanthropist opened a museum in Malibu, California.
— J. Paul Getty.

Rembrandt's *The Night Watch* is exhibited in this Dutch museum.
— Rijk's Museum, Amsterdam.

Where is the Freer Gallery?
— Washington, D. C.

Where are these museums?

Museum	City
Victoria and Albert	London
Museum of Modern Art	New York
Imperial Palace Museum	Beijing
Sumo Museum	Tokyo
Napoleonic Museum	Rome
Red Cross Museum	Geneva

In England, Oxford University's Ashmolean Museum was designed by...?
— Charles Robert Cockerell.

With more than 140 million items in 16 museums, this complex (the world's largest) was founded in 1846.
— The Smithsonian, in Washington, D.C. Besides the National Gallery of Art and the National Portrait Gallery, it encompasses the Cooper-Hewitt Museum of Decorative Arts and Design, in New York City. The John F. Kennedy Center for the Performing Arts is an independent bureau of the institution.

This complex in Berlin has the Pergamon and Bode Museums.
— Museum Island.

This Ottawa art museum moved into a permanent residence in 1988.
— The National Gallery of Canada.

The Norsk Folk Museum in this capital of Norway has some 150 recreated native structures from across the country.
— Oslo.

What American gallery has the largest collection of mobiles by Alexander Calder?
— The Whitney Museum of American Art, in New York City.

Begun by Russia's Catherine the Great, this museum in St. Petersburg is one of the world's foremost houses of art.

— The Hermitage, in St. Petersburg (Leningrad)

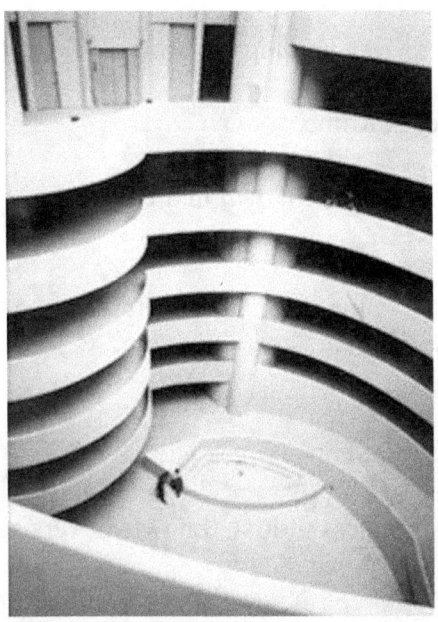

Completed in 1959, this circular Frank Lloyd Wright-designed museum in New York includes works by Brancusi and Kandinsky.
— The Solomon R. Guggenheim Museum.

Frank Lloyd Wright's Guggenheim

Sculptors

Michelangelo's statue of Mary holding the dead body of
Jesus is called...?
— *The Pietá*, in St. Peter's, Rome.

This Florentine created his bronze *David* in the 1430s.
— Donatello.

Lord Elgin gave his name to the group of sculptures he
took to London from the...?
— Parthenon.

The Venus de Milo, discovered on a Greek isle called
Milos in 1820, is a statue of...?
— Aphrodite, the Greek goddess of love (known as Venus
to the Romans.)

The Quadriga of Victory statue atop Berlin's Brandenburg
Gate is a sculptured...?
— Chariot.

The *Minuteman* statue, his first, led to many commissions,
including the heroic figure of Abraham Lincoln in the
Lincoln Memorial.
— Daniel Chester French (1850-1931).

This sculptor of *Bronco Buster* studied at Yale and the Art
Students League of New York.
— Frederick Remington.

This sculptor of Western Americana designed the Indian head nickel in 1913.
— James Earle Fraser.

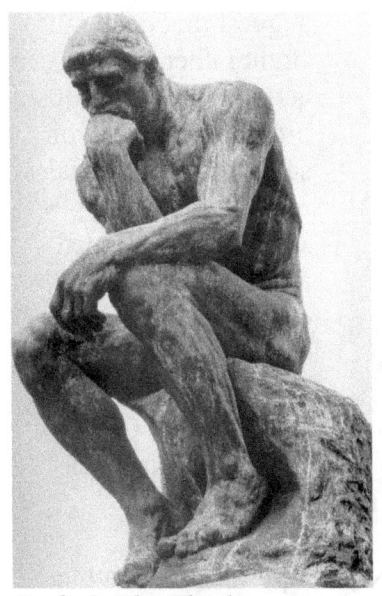

Rodin's The Thinker

This Rodin work was conceived to top his *Gate of Hell*.
— *The Thinker.*

A famous monument to Honoré Balzac (now in the Sculpture Garden of the New York Museum of Modern Art) and *The Burghers of Calais* were sculpted by...?
— Auguste Rodin (1840-1917.) He also sculpted George Bernard Shaw and Victor Hugo.

Around 1928, this English sculptor gained international repute. He worked in wood, stone, and cement to create smooth organic shapes, incorporating empty hollows as points of interest. His favorite subjects were reclining figures and mother-and-child compositions.
— Henry Moore.

White plaster human figures in everyday settings brought attention to this Pop Art sculptor.
— George Segal (born N.Y.C. 1924)

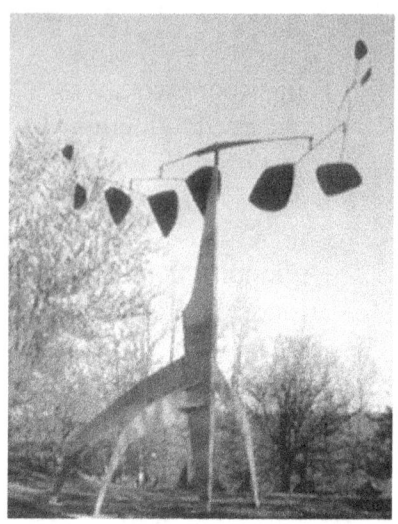

Calder's Southern Cross, 1963

Taking his cue from the Fauves, Constantin Brancusi cast his bronze *Bird in Space*, 1928, to suggest the *feeling* of flight rather than an actual bird. The 1930s brought wrought-iron sculptor Julio Gonzales to the fore, and <u>this</u> American developed mobile sculptures of delicately balanced constructions hung on metal wires.
— Alexander Calder, called, by Miró, "the tough guy with the soul of a nightingale."

"Primary Structures," relatively simple shapes on a huge scale, were pioneered by German sculptor Mathias Goeritz in Mexico City in the 1950s. American David Smith's *Cubi* series, in stainless steel, puts cubes and cylinders in dynamic juxtaposition on a grand scale. In <u>this</u> man's unique application of the Primary Structure, bulldozers were used to construct his *Spiral Jetty*, which extended into Utah's Great Salt Lake.
— Robert Smithson.

This artist's monumental structures originate in objects of everyday use. His *Giant Ice Bag* was displayed at the US Pavilion at EXPO 70 in Osaka, Japan.
— Claes Oldenberg.

Seven Wonders of the Ancient World

Erected around 280 BC, this statue of the Sun God was as tall as the Statue of Liberty.
— The Colossus of Rhodes.

This ancient wonder was a marble tomb.
— The Mausoleum at Halicarnassus.

The Great Pyramid of Cheops (Khufu) is in…?
— Egypt.

The Hanging Gardens were in...?
— Babylon (now Iraq.)

The Temple of Artemis (the Artemision) at Ephesis is in...?
— Turkey.

The Statue of Zeus (by Phidias) at Olympia...?
— Greece.

The Lighthouse of Pharos...?
— Near Alexandria, Egypt. (Some include the walls of Babylon in its place.)

If you've found this book useful, please consider leaving a short review on Amazon. Thank you.

KNOWLEDGE *BLASTER!* Series of educational study guides:

American History
Art History
Food and Drink
Geography and Travel
Literature
Movies
Music
Mythology
Sports
Weight Training and Total Fitness
World History

Yucca Road Productions